Prayers & Meditations for Children

Discarded by MVCL

Antonia Felix

Illustrations by Patricia Shen

This edition published in 1997 by SMITHMARK Publishers, a division of U.S. Media Holdings, Inc., 115 West 18th Street, New York, NY 10011.

SMITHMARK books are available for bulk purchase for sales promotion and premium use. For details write or call the manager of special sales, SMITHMARK Publishers, 115 West 18th Street, New York, NY 10011.

This book was designed and produced by Todtri Productions Limited P.O. Box 572, New York, NY 10116-0572 FAX: (212) 695-6688

Printed and bound in Hong Kong

Library of Congress Catalog Card Number 97-066068
ISBN 0-7651-9198-9

Author: Antonia Felix
Illustrator: Patricia Shea

Publisher: Robert M. Tod
Editorial Director: Elizabeth Loonan
Senior Editor: Cynthia Sternau
Project Editor: Ann Kirby
Production Coordinator: Jay Weiser
Designer: Betty Barnstable

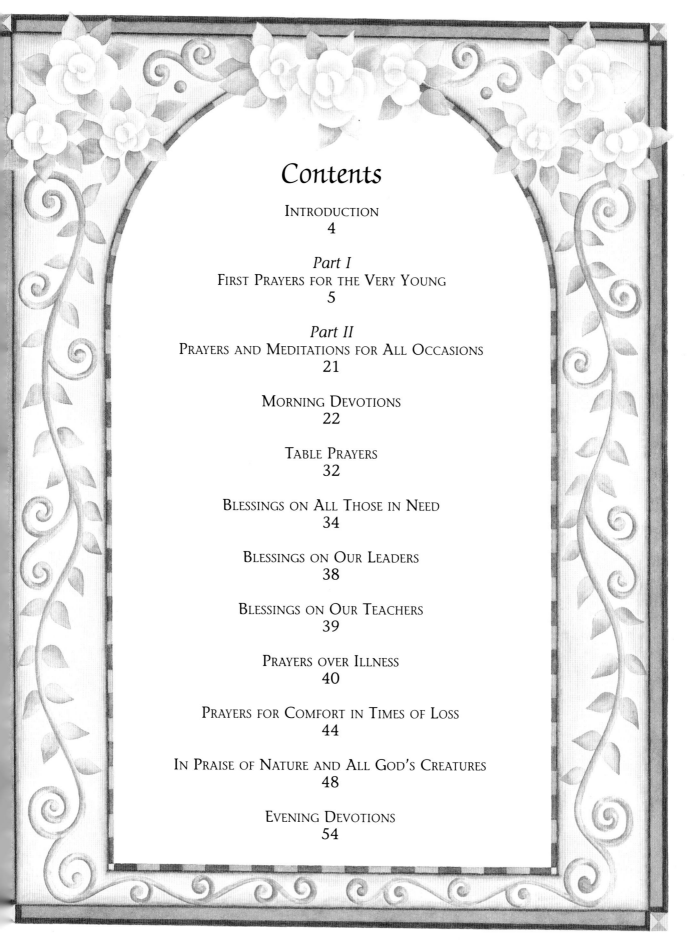

Contents

INTRODUCTION

It is never too early to begin to nurture the spiritual path and to discover the comfort and benefit of prayer. Devotions have played an important role in families for many generations, often supported by prayerbooks that supplement the Bible and other sacred writings. In the spirit of this time-honored tradition, this little volume of prayers and meditations for children opens the way to an understanding of faith on both a personal and a universal level.

Charming borders and illustrations frame and illuminate a selection of simple prayers, biblical quotations, poems, and meditations. Many prayers originated in the nineteenth century in an era when prayerbooks flourished, as home devotions formed a sustaining bond within families in America and Europe.

The book opens with "First Prayers for the Very Young," a collection of familiar, easy-to-memorize verses. The rest of the prayerbook is divided into themes, designed to allow the parent or child to choose a topic for the day's reading which reflects events or a need for understanding pertaining to their own lives.

The invitation to open young hearts to God is the greatest joy of parenthood, and it is to parents everywhere this book is lovingly dedicated.

Children are a gift from God.
—Psalms 127:3

PART I
FIRST PRAYERS FOR THE VERY YOUNG

These short and simple prayers introduce the very young to our most personal ritual of folded hands. Learned at a tender age, these bedtime prayers, table graces, and biblical verses will remain in the heart for a lifetime.

*T*his is the day the Lord has made,

Let us rejoice and be glad in it!

–Psalms 118:24

God is great, God is good;
Let us thank Him for our food,
Amen.

I'm glad my blessed Savior
Was once a child like me,
To show how pure and holy
His little ones might be:
And if I try to follow
His footsteps here below,
He never will forget me
Because He loves me so.

Direct me in your ways, God, and teach me your paths.

–Psalms 25:4

THE LORD'S PRAYER

Our Father, who art in Heaven, hallowed be
Thy name. Thy kingdom come, Thy will be
done on earth as it is in Heaven. Give us this
day our daily bread. Forgive us our trespasses,
as we forgive those who trespass against us.
And lead us not into temptation, but deliver
us from evil. For Thine is the
kingdom, the power, and the
glory. For ever and ever.

Amen.

*B*lessed are the peacemakers, for they shall be called the children of God.

—Matthew 5:9

Glory to God in the highest, and peace to His people on earth.

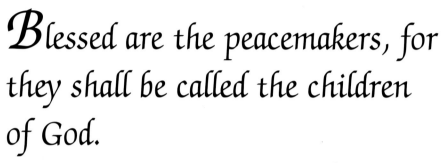

Holy Spirit, help us
Daily by Thy might,
What is wrong to conquer,
And to choose the right.

Little deeds of kindness,
Little words of love;
Make our earth an Eden,
Like the Heaven above.

Dear Lord, I love You.
Help me to love You better, and to
love everyone in your creation.

Praise God, from whom all blessings flow;

Praise Him, all creatures here below;

Praise Him above, ye heavenly host;

Praise Father, Son, and Holy Ghost.

Amen.

*H*onor your father and
your mother.

—Exodus 20:12

Fill my heart with true
love for You, dear God. Thank
You for the gift of love and
for my family.

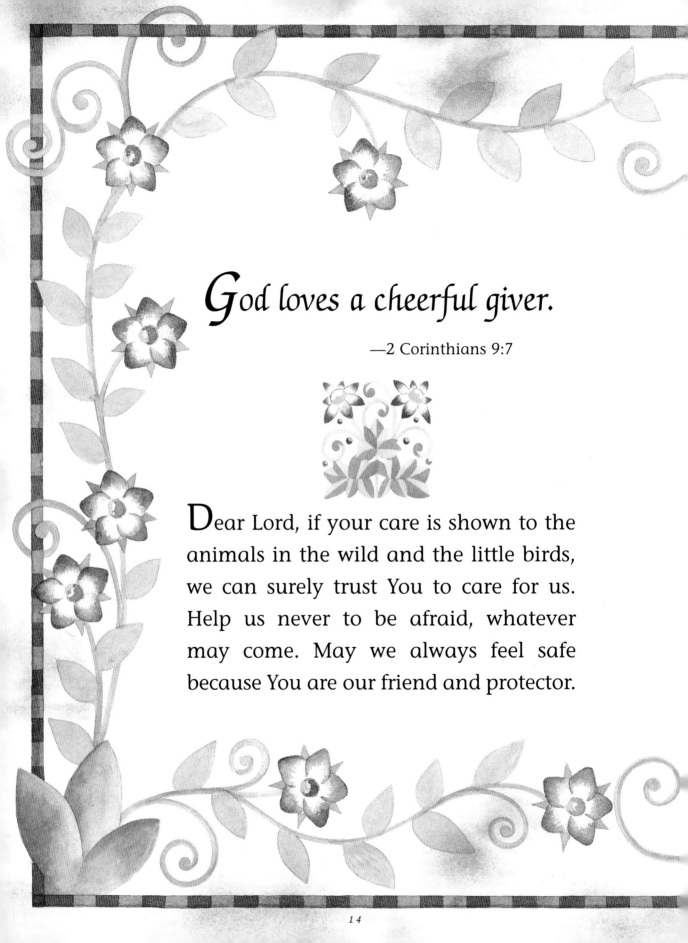

God loves a cheerful giver.

—2 Corinthians 9:7

Dear Lord, if your care is shown to the animals in the wild and the little birds, we can surely trust You to care for us. Help us never to be afraid, whatever may come. May we always feel safe because You are our friend and protector.

And you shall love the Lord your God with all your heart and with all your soul, and with all your mind, and with all your strength.

—Mark 12:30

Dear God, teach me something to do for You today. May I always be ready to help others.

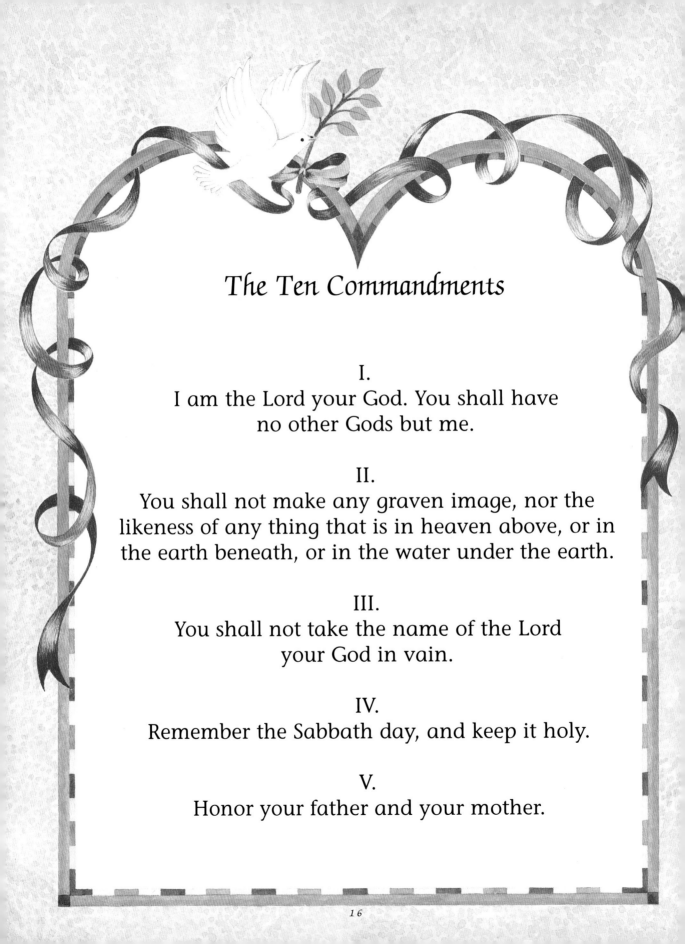

The Ten Commandments

I.
I am the Lord your God. You shall have
no other Gods but me.

II.
You shall not make any graven image, nor the
likeness of any thing that is in heaven above, or in
the earth beneath, or in the water under the earth.

III.
You shall not take the name of the Lord
your God in vain.

IV.
Remember the Sabbath day, and keep it holy.

V.
Honor your father and your mother.

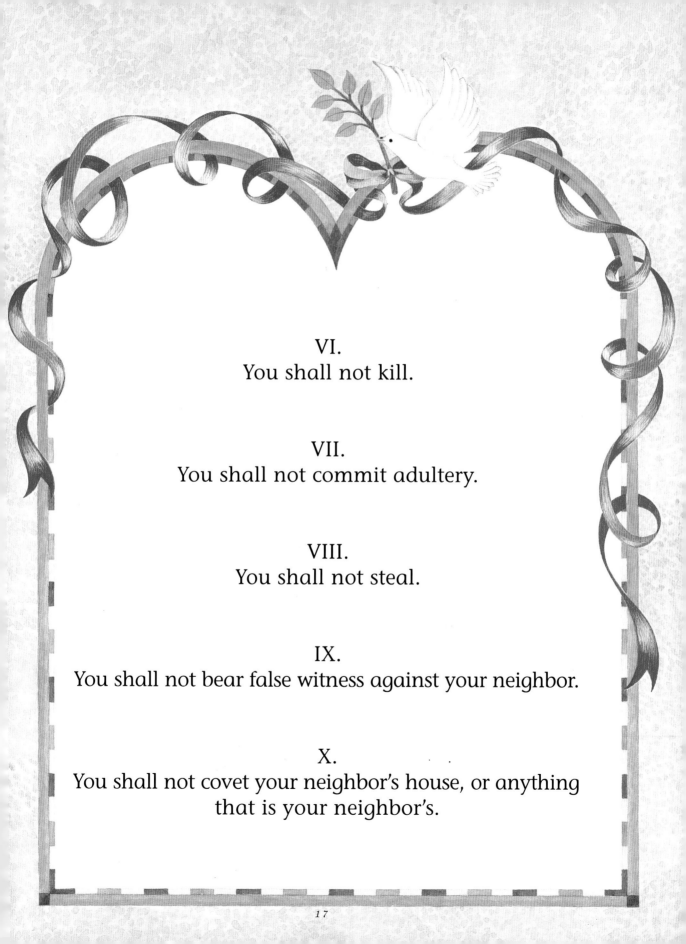

VI.
You shall not kill.

VII.
You shall not commit adultery.

VIII.
You shall not steal.

IX.
You shall not bear false witness against your neighbor.

X.
You shall not covet your neighbor's house, or anything
that is your neighbor's.

Dear God in Heaven, thank You
for taking care of me today. Bless my
father and my mother, and all my family.
Let me sleep safely in your love tonight.
Amen.

Now I lay me down to sleep,
I pray thee, Lord, my soul to keep.
If I should die before I wake,
I pray thee, Lord, my soul to take.

*Draw near to God
and He will draw near to you.*

—James 4:8

God is everywhere. He is in Heaven. He is on earth. He sees all things. He hears all things. I am sure he hears every word we say. I will pray to be made a good child. Good night!

Ask, and ye shall receive,
that your joy may be full.

—John 16:24

PART II
PRAYERS AND MEDITATIONS
FOR ALL OCCASIONS

It is wonderful to begin the day thinking about God, to ask for His inspiration and support in everything we do, and to whisper thanks to the Lord before we close our eyes in sleep. Whether we are happy, thankful, concerned for someone, or even sad, God is listening to our thoughts and feeling what is in our hearts. For every event that comes into our lives, God offers love and understanding.

MORNING DEVOTIONS

*T*each me, my God and King, in all things Thee to see, and what I do in anything, to do it as for Thee.

Eternal God, Heavenly Father, the author and preserver of our lives, we thank You that You permit us to see the light of another day, and we beseech You to continue to give us your merciful protection. Give to each one of us, O Lord, a clear knowledge of our duties and responsibilities, and endue us with wisdom and strength from on high that we may discharge them this day with cheerfulness.

Almighty and gracious God, who now at the return of day has displayed your goodness and power in restoring strength to our bodies and light to our eyes, hear these words of love and thanksgiving. Take away from us all ignorance, that we may know both ourselves and You. Continue to give us your precious gifts and blessings, in body, mind, and soul, with grace to use them ever in your service, to your honor and glory.

A loyal friend is something beyond price, there is no measuring his worth.

—Ecclesiastics 6:15

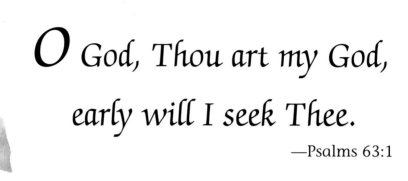

*O God, Thou art my God,
early will I seek Thee.*

—Psalms 63:1

Almighty God, who has preserved me through the past night, I pray to You to continue to watch over me through the coming day, and to bless my parents, brothers, sisters, and friends, as well as myself, and to keep us all in goodness and safety and make us truly thankful for all your great goodness and mercy. I will try, Lord, with your blessing, to pass this day without doing wrong. Amen.

O Lord, who took up little children in your arms and blessed them, look down graciously on us and bless us also. Give me a new heart, that I may praise You for all your goodness to me, and that I may love and serve You all the days of my life. In all I do, and speak, and think today, may I remember that You, O Lord, see me.

Holy Spirit, give us
   Each a humble mind,
Make us more like Jesus,
   Gentle, pure, and kind.

Holy Spirit, brighten
   Little deeds of toil,
And our playful pastimes
   Let no folly spoil.

Holy Spirit, help us
   Daily by Thy might,
What is wrong to conquer,
   And to choose the right.

I pray you, God, lover of Earth's children,

that my little life may come to bless your world.

Most glorious Lord, I offer You my thanks this morning, for all the blessings of the past night. The sleep with which I have been refreshed, the light of returning day, and health to use and enjoy it are all your gifts.

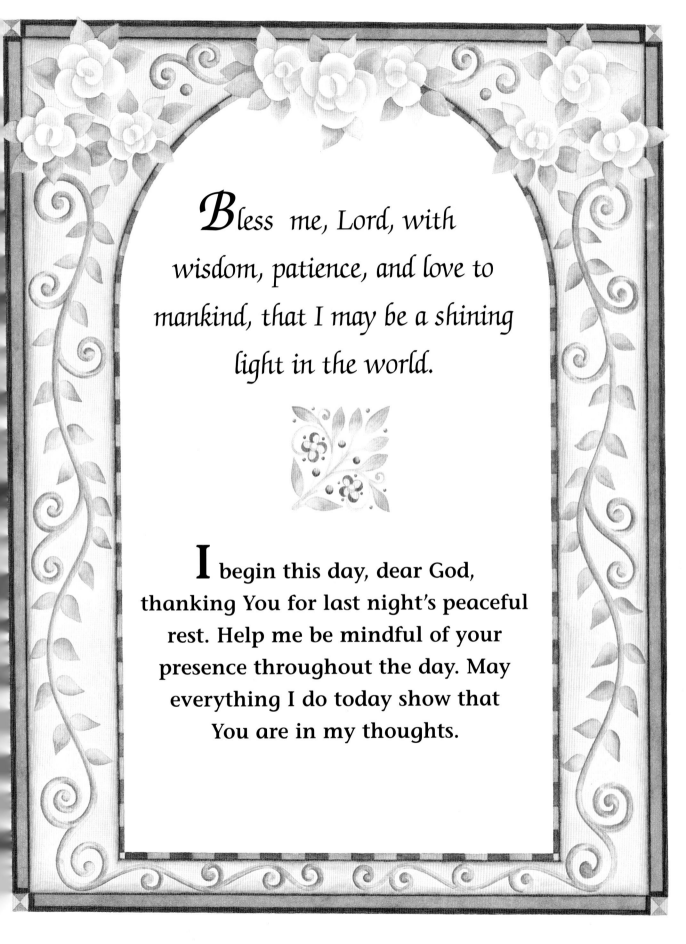

Bless me, Lord, with wisdom, patience, and love to mankind, that I may be a shining light in the world.

I begin this day, dear God, thanking You for last night's peaceful rest. Help me be mindful of your presence throughout the day. May everything I do today show that You are in my thoughts.

The day returns and brings me work and play. Dear God, fill me with the love of learning, that my lessons today may bring me the joy of discovering more about your world.

Praised be my Lord God with all His creatures, and especially our brother the sun, who brings us the day and who brings us the light; fair is he and shines with a great splendor; O Lord, to us he signifies You.

I will lift up mine eyes unto the hills, from whence cometh my help. My help cometh from the Lord, which made heaven and earth.

—Psalms 121:1,2

Maker of the universe, as the day returns, return to us, our sun and comforter. Call us up with morning faces and with morning hearts, eager to be happy. If this day brings problems or challenges, remind us that You are always with us. If this day should be marked with sorrow, make us strong to endure it.

Love your neighbor as yourself.

—Mark 12:31

Dear Lord, in your holy word You teach us that any one who needs our help is our neighbor. To care for another person as for ourselves, to be ready to deny ourselves something in order to give to someone else, seems very hard, until we remember that all kindness shown another is kindness shown to You. This thought makes us willing and glad to do anything, because it is done for You.

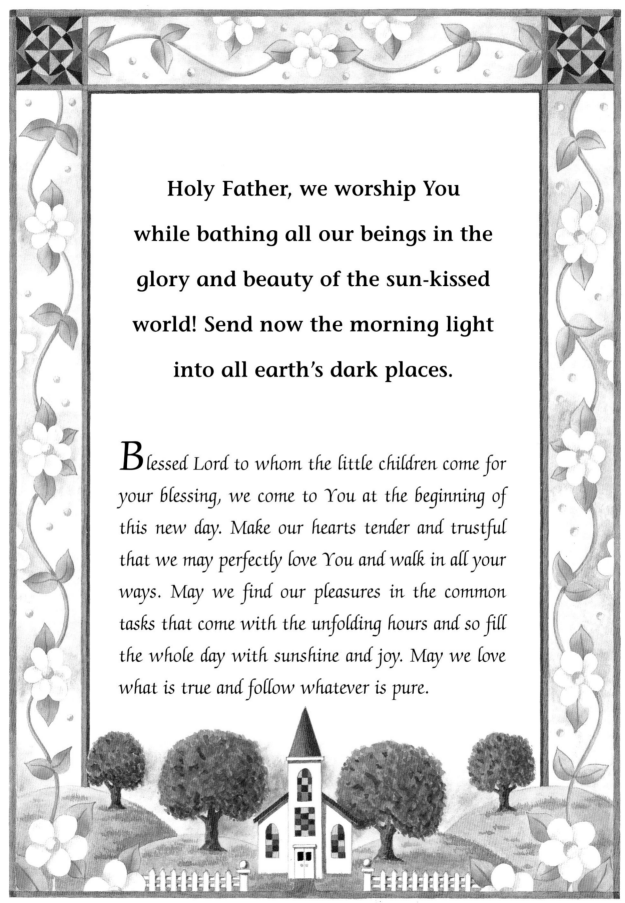

Holy Father, we worship You while bathing all our beings in the glory and beauty of the sun-kissed world! Send now the morning light into all earth's dark places.

Blessed Lord to whom the little children come for your blessing, we come to You at the beginning of this new day. Make our hearts tender and trustful that we may perfectly love You and walk in all your ways. May we find our pleasures in the common tasks that come with the unfolding hours and so fill the whole day with sunshine and joy. May we love what is true and follow whatever is pure.

TABLE PRAYERS

Lord, behold our family gathered
here. We thank You for this place in
which we live, for the love that unites
us, for the peace given us this day,
for the hope which we hold for
tomorrow, for the health, the work,
the food, and the friendships that
make our lives delightful.

Amen.

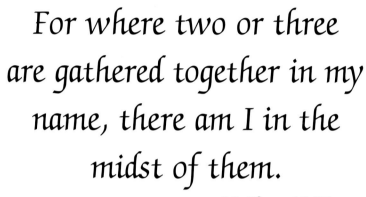

For where two or three are gathered together in my name, there am I in the midst of them.

—Matthew 18:20

*B*less, O Lord, this food to my use, and let it strengthen me for Thy service.

Amen.

*B*less, O Lord, the food we are going to share, and make us truly thankful for this and every comfort we receive.

Amen.

BLESSINGS ON ALL THOSE IN NEED

In the time of my trouble I called upon the Lord, and the Lord heard me.

Loving and all-knowing God, have mercy on all who are troubled. May they not be cast down; support the stumbling on the way, and give rest to the weary.

O dear Lord, we long to think less of ourselves, and more of others. Take our hearts, we pray, and fill them so full of your love that we will try every day to do all we can to make those about us happy.

Bring your blessings, Lord, to the people in nations which are visited by war, and bring them food, safety, healing, and peace.

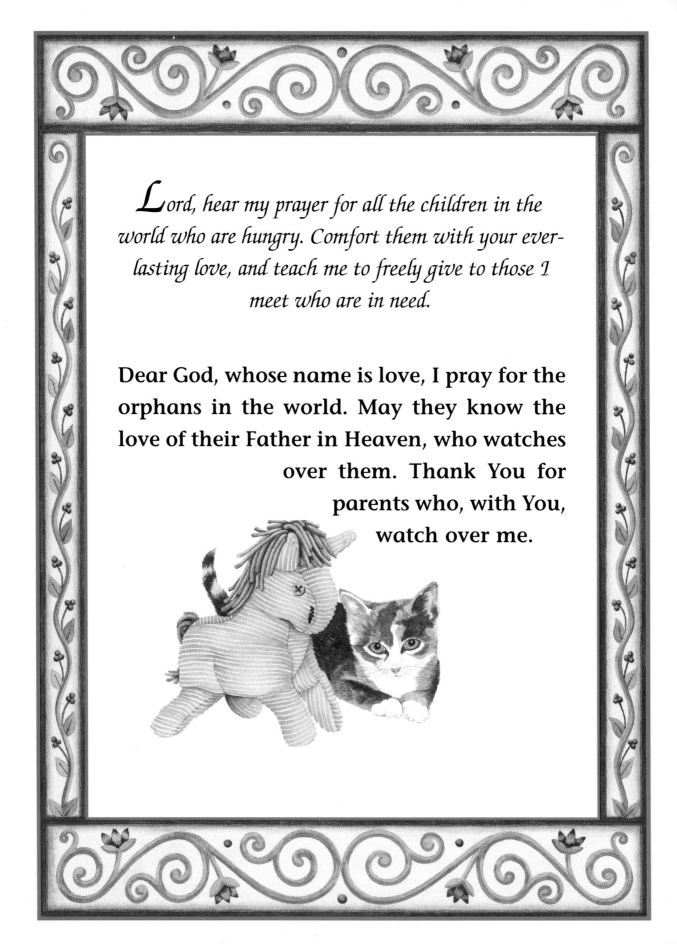

Lord, hear my prayer for all the children in the world who are hungry. Comfort them with your everlasting love, and teach me to freely give to those I meet who are in need.

Dear God, whose name is love, I pray for the orphans in the world. May they know the love of their Father in Heaven, who watches over them. Thank You for parents who, with You, watch over me.

 **Look,** dear Lord, in mercy upon all suffering people. Be the widow's protector, the orphan's parent, the prisoner's companion, the sick man's physician, the afflicted man's comforter, the poor man's friend. And may all the troubles of the distressed cause them to listen to the voice of that gracious Savior, who invites the weary and heavy laden to come unto him.

BLESSINGS ON OUR LEADERS

Let brotherly love continue.

—Hebrews 13:1

Grant, dear Lord, that all those who govern, including the President of the United States, may know and love your truth. Bless them with wisdom, patience, zeal, humility, and love to mankind that they may be burning and shining lights in the world.

BLESSINGS ON OUR TEACHERS

Heavenly Father, endue all teachers of youth in schools with understanding, patience, and love. May they advance the causes of learning and godly discipline, and prepare the rising generation to live virtuous, honorable, and useful lives.

Source of wisdom, let those who teach
be precious in your sight. Thank You
for granting them patience and kindness
in bringing instruction to your children.

PRAYERS OVER ILLNESS

He nurses them when they are sick, and soothes all their pains and worries.

—Psalms 41:3

O Father of mercies, and God of all comfort, our only help in time of need, look down from heaven, we humbly beseech You, and behold, visit, and relieve your sick child. Comfort me with a sense of your goodness, give me patience during my illness, and, in your good time, restore me to health.

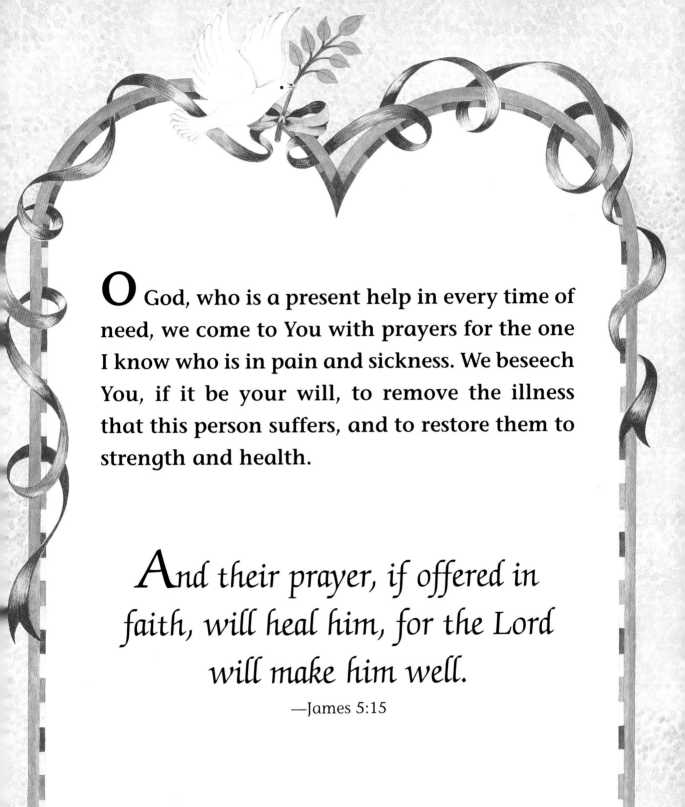

O God, who is a present help in every time of need, we come to You with prayers for the one I know who is in pain and sickness. We beseech You, if it be your will, to remove the illness that this person suffers, and to restore them to strength and health.

And their prayer, if offered in faith, will heal him, for the Lord will make him well.

—James 5:15

*A*nd we know that all
things work together for good
to them that love God.

—Romans 8:28

Almighty God who helps and comforts all who are in sickness or sorrow, I pray You to bestow your blessing upon my dear friend, to shorten his time of suffering, and to restore him speedily to health. May he be full of thankfulness for your great kindness and mercy.

PRAYERS FOR COMFORT IN TIMES OF LOSS

When God's creatures die,
God sends His angels for them, and takes
them to Heaven. Everything that breathes
sings its song of love for God. Every
heart is precious in His sight.

Jesus said:
Peace I bequeath to you,
my own peace I give,
a peace which the world cannot give,
this is my gift to you.
—John 14:27

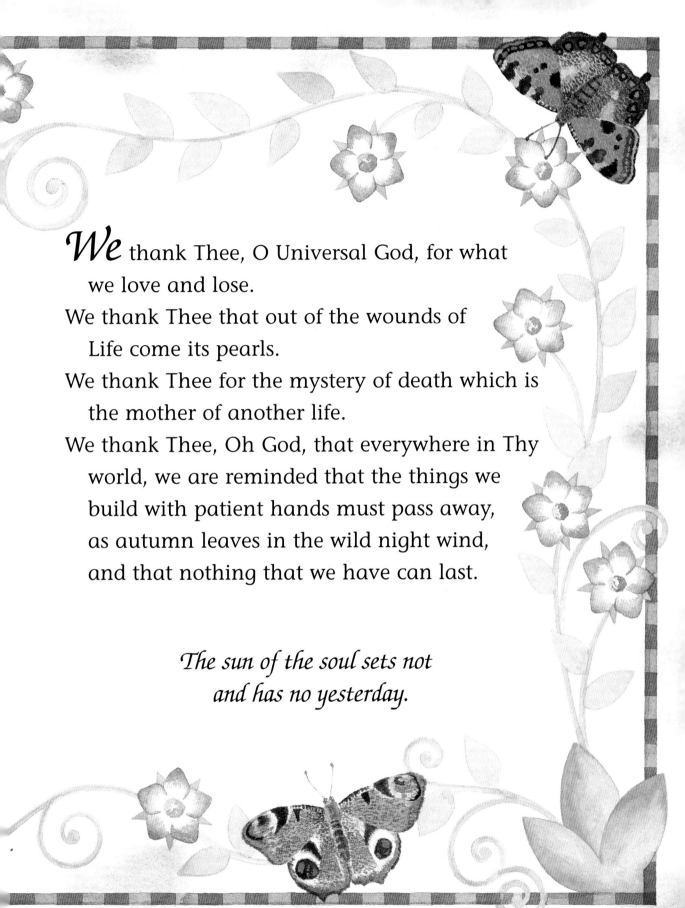

We thank Thee, O Universal God, for what we love and lose.

We thank Thee that out of the wounds of Life come its pearls.

We thank Thee for the mystery of death which is the mother of another life.

We thank Thee, Oh God, that everywhere in Thy world, we are reminded that the things we build with patient hands must pass away, as autumn leaves in the wild night wind, and that nothing that we have can last.

*The sun of the soul sets not
and has no yesterday.*

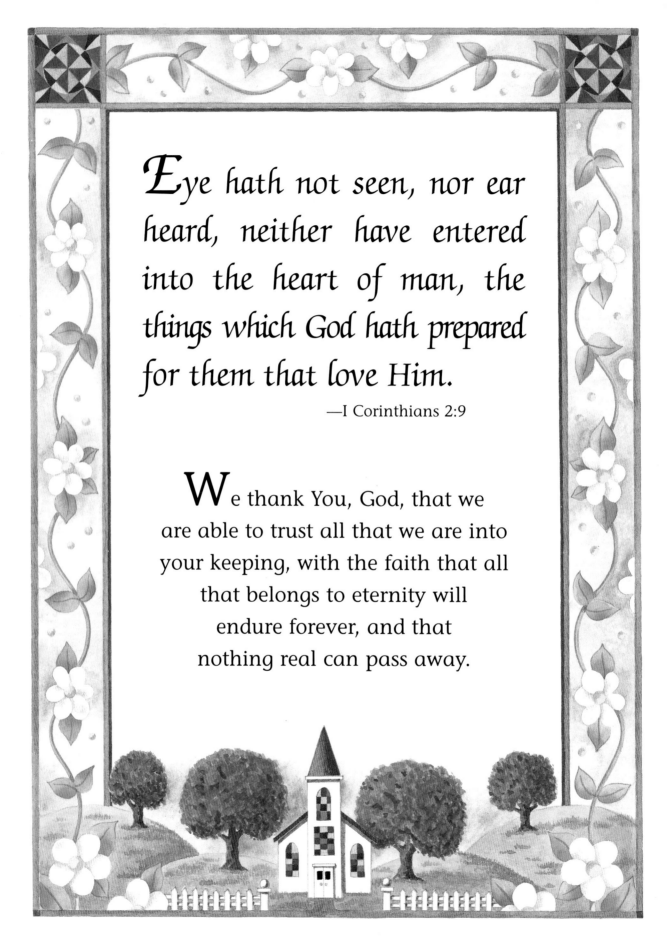

Eye hath not seen, nor ear heard, neither have entered into the heart of man, the things which God hath prepared for them that love Him.

—I Corinthians 2:9

We thank You, God, that we are able to trust all that we are into your keeping, with the faith that all that belongs to eternity will endure forever, and that nothing real can pass away.

Dear heavenly Father, who alone can heal the wounds of this life, hear my prayer. In this time of sadness, fill me with your peace which passes all understanding.

If there be in front of us any painful duty,
strengthen us with the grace of courage. Let us
not lose the savor of past mercies and past pleasures,
but, like the voice of a bird singing in
the rain, let grateful memory survive
in the hour of darkness.

IN PRAISE OF NATURE
AND ALL GOD'S CREATURES

Show love to all creatures, and you will be happy; for when you love all things, you love the Lord, for He is all in all.

Dear Lord, a thousand streams run free
    By sunny banks of wood and wild
This day, to shine and work for Thee:
    And I am but a little child:
Yet help me, in my work and play,
To do Thy will as well as they.

Teach us, Lord, the meaning of the rain and trees and fishes. Let us see ourselves for what we are, one out of the countless number of the clans of Thy handiwork.

All things bright and beautiful,
   all creatures great and small,
All things wise and wonderful,
   the Lord God made them all.
Each little flower that opens,
   each little bird that sings,
He made their glowing colors,
He made their tiny wings.

*H*e cuts out rivers among the
rocks, and His eye sees every
precious thing.

—Job 28:10

O God, help me to be gentle and merciful to all the creatures which You have made; may I never be cruel in word or act, remembering your kindness to all.

This is my Father's world,
and to my listening ears
all nature sings and round me rings
the music of the spheres.
This is my Father's world:
I rest me in the thought
of rocks and trees, of skies
  and seas,
His hand the wonders wrought.

All creatures of our God and King,
Lift up your voice and with us sing
Alleluia, Alleluia!
Thou burning sun with golden beam,
Thou silver moon with softer gleam,
O praise Him, O praise Him
Alleluia, Alleluia, Alleluia!

Dear God, we adore You in the beauty of the grass and the flowers, in the sweetness of the air and the precious rain that falls. We glorify You in the love we have for our pets, our special friends whom You have lovingly placed in our lives.

Great and glorious Lord our God, before the mountains were brought forth, before You had formed the world, from everlasting to everlasting, You are God. The things which our eyes behold shall perish, but You shall endure. The things of this earth shall change, as do the passing seasons, but You are the same, and your years shall have no end.

EVENING DEVOTIONS

Now the day is over, night is drawing nigh,
shadows of the evening steal across the sky.
Jesus, give the weary calm and sweet repose;
with thy tenderest blessing may our eyelids close.

To your loving protection I humbly commit myself and all my friends this night. Bestow the best blessings of Heaven and earth on my dear father and mother and all my dear relations. Refresh my wearied limbs with sleep, and grant, that when the morning shall again dawn upon me, the eyes of my soul may be opened by the renewed light of your grace.

The day is done, and the darkness
Falls from the wings of night,
As a feather is wafted downward
From an eagle in his flight.

And the night shall be filled with music,
And the cares that infest the day,
Shall fold their tents, like the Arabs,
And as silently steal away.

O Lord, You are my father in heaven. Help me now to pray. I thank You for life, and health, and food, and clothes. I thank You for home, and friends, and all the blessings of this day. O Lord, pardon all my sins. Forgive all I have done wrong this day. Make me a good child. Make me like the Lord Jesus. Give me your Holy Spirit to make me holy.
Amen.

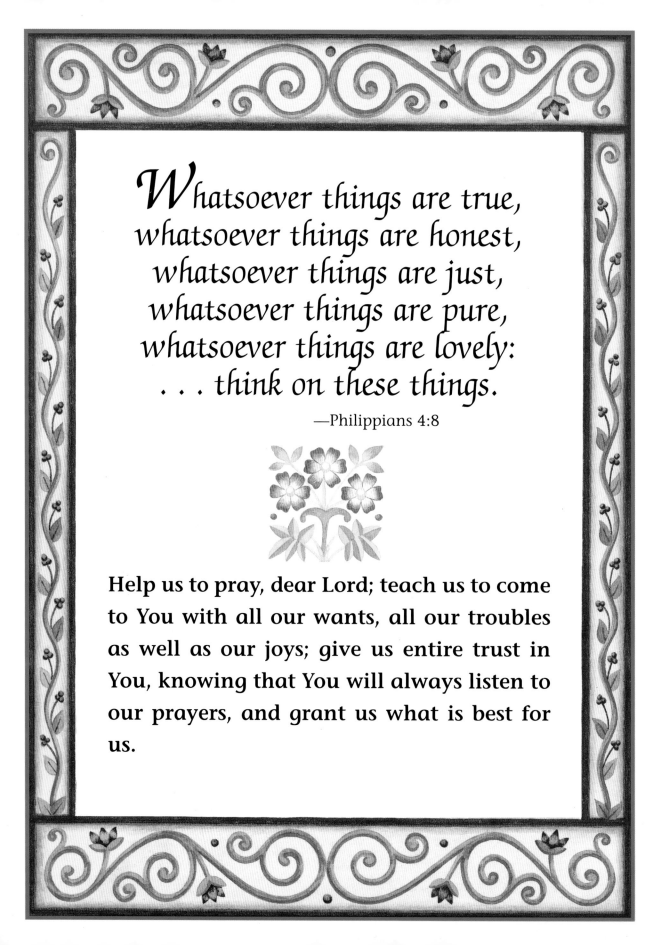

*W*hatsoever things are true, whatsoever things are honest, whatsoever things are just, whatsoever things are pure, whatsoever things are lovely: . . . think on these things.

—Philippians 4:8

Help us to pray, dear Lord; teach us to come to You with all our wants, all our troubles as well as our joys; give us entire trust in You, knowing that You will always listen to our prayers, and grant us what is best for us.

O God, now while I am still a child I give You my heart; take it, I pray, into your own care and keeping, that through my whole life I may belong to You.

All praise to Thee, my God, this night,
for all the blessings of the light:
keep me, O keep me, King of kings,
beneath Thine own almighty wings.

O may my soul on Thee repose,
and with sweet sleep mine eyelids close;
sleep that shall me more vigorous make
to serve my God when I awake.

And be ye kind to one another, tender-hearted, forgiving one another, even as God, for Christ's sake, hath forgiven you.

—Ephesians 4:32

Thou, who art God of the sunset and the dawn, we thank Thee for the chances we have had today to love thy world and to be kind, and we pray that the chances we have lost today may not be lost tomorrow.

We thank You, God, for the sweet
gift of love, and that You,
who made the earth and the stars,
should care for us.

We are sleeping tonight under
your sky and in the shelter of your
love—and all is well.

Goodnight, Oh God, to your world
and our thanks and our love
to You.

*H*e that doeth good is of God.

—3 John 1:11

O God, my heavenly Father, who has promised your children the Holy Spirit, pour down this blessing upon me, that my heart may be prepared to offer up to You my evening prayer. O God, who knows my heart, forgive me for everything I have done today that may have brought sadness or anger to anyone. Fill me with your Holy Spirit that I may always obey your greatest commandment, to love others.

May we always remember, dear God, that any work done well, no matter what the work may be, at home or at school, all is work done for You, if we try to put love for You into what we do.

Now, O Lord, our ever watchful guardian, please take us and all belonging to us under your care this night, that we may rest in peace, and wake in health and safety.

The Lord is good to all,
and His tender mercies are over
all His works.

—Psalms 145:9

Often when we try to pray to You, dear Lord, our thoughts wander, and we think of many little things which have nothing to do with our prayer. At those times, we feel that if we could see You near us, we would not let other thoughts interrupt our prayer. Help us to realize that although our eyes cannot see You, You are right by our side.

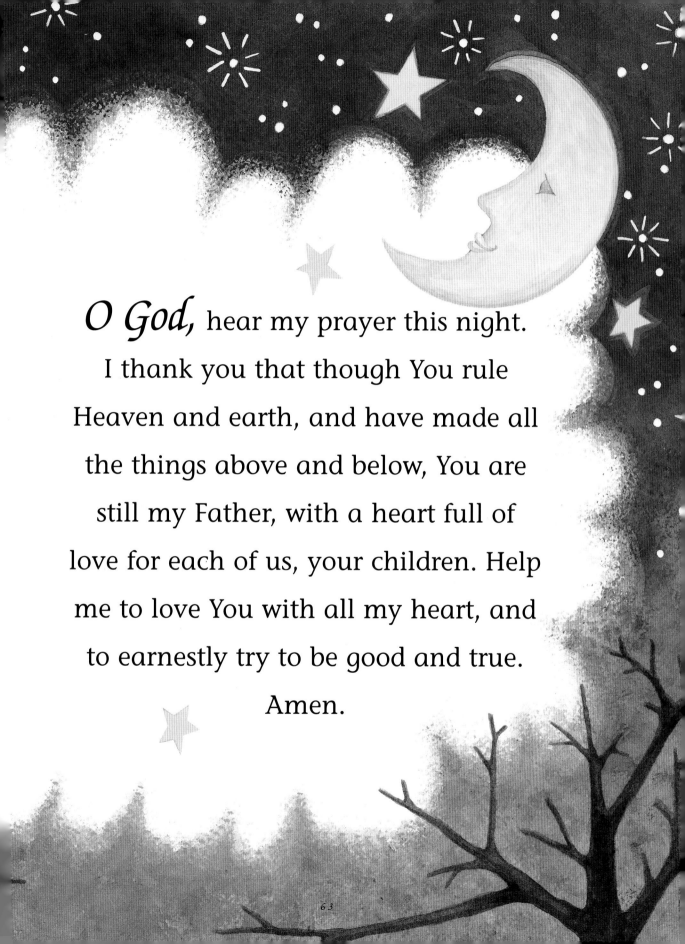

O God, hear my prayer this night. I thank you that though You rule Heaven and earth, and have made all the things above and below, You are still my Father, with a heart full of love for each of us, your children. Help me to love You with all my heart, and to earnestly try to be good and true.

Amen.

Let the little children come to me, and do not stop them; for it is to such as these that the kingdom of God belongs.

—Luke 18:16

O God, we need your help every moment of our lives; to watch over us at night while we sleep, and to keep us from harm during the day. Help us to be thankful to You for all your watchful care, and to try with all our might, with your help, to do what is right.